Money on Your Mind

Money on Your Mind

Matthew Petchinsky

1

Money on Your Mind: A Beginner's Guide to Wealth

By: Matthew Petchinsky

Introduction

Financial literacy is the cornerstone of personal empowerment and the gateway to creating lasting wealth. In an ever-evolving global economy, understanding money—how it works, how to manage it, and how to make it grow—has never been more critical. Yet, for many, financial literacy is a skill learned too late or not at all, leaving individuals vulnerable to debt, financial insecurity, and missed opportunities. This introduction explores why financial literacy is essential and provides a roadmap for building wealth from the ground up, no matter your starting point.

Why Financial Literacy Matters

At its core, financial literacy is the ability to understand and effectively use various financial skills, including budgeting, investing, and saving. It encompasses the knowledge necessary to make informed and confident financial decisions that align with one's goals and values. Here's why it matters:

1. **Empowers Decision-Making**
   Financial literacy equips you with the tools to make informed choices about spending, saving, and investing. Whether deciding on a mortgage, planning for retirement, or navigating daily expenses, being financially literate helps you weigh your options and choose wisely.
2. **Builds Resilience Against Financial Crises**
   Life is unpredictable, and financial emergencies can strike at any time. Financial literacy prepares you to handle these challenges with an emergency fund, insurance, and a solid understanding of credit management.
3. **Breaks the Cycle of Poverty**
   For many, financial illiteracy perpetuates a cycle of poverty. Understanding financial basics, such as compound interest and bud-

geting, can empower individuals to escape this cycle and build a stable future for themselves and their families.

4. **Facilitates Long-Term Wealth Building**
   Knowing how to invest wisely, manage debt, and save for the future lays the groundwork for financial independence and generational wealth.
5. **Navigates an Increasingly Complex Financial World**
   From understanding cryptocurrencies to interpreting tax laws, the financial landscape is more complex than ever. Financial literacy helps you stay informed and adapt to these changes.

How to Create Wealth from the Ground Up

Creating wealth is a journey that requires discipline, knowledge, and a long-term vision. While everyone's path may look different, the principles of wealth creation remain universal. Here are the key steps to building wealth, even from humble beginnings:

1. **Master the Basics: Budgeting and Saving**
   The foundation of wealth creation starts with managing your income effectively. Budgeting ensures you allocate your resources wisely, prioritizing essentials while setting aside money for savings and investments. Start with the 50/30/20 rule: allocate 50% of your income to needs, 30% to wants, and 20% to savings and debt repayment.
2. **Eliminate Debt**
   High-interest debt is one of the biggest barriers to wealth. Focus on paying down debts, especially credit cards and personal loans, as quickly as possible. Use strategies like the snowball or avalanche method to reduce debt systematically.
3. **Build an Emergency Fund**
   Before investing, ensure you have a safety net. An emergency fund should cover three to six months of essential expenses, providing security against unexpected costs such as medical bills or job loss.
4. **Invest Early and Consistently**
   Time is your greatest ally in building wealth. Start investing as early as possible, even in small amounts. Take advantage of compounding returns by consistently contributing to retirement accounts, stocks, or other investment vehicles.
5. **Diversify Income Streams**
   Relying solely on one source of income can be risky. Consider building multiple income streams, such as side hustles, rental income, or dividend-paying investments.

6. **Educate Yourself on Wealth-Building Strategies**
   Knowledge is power. Read books, attend seminars, and learn from successful investors to deepen your understanding of financial strategies. Knowledge not only empowers but also mitigates the risks of poor decisions.
7. **Adopt a Growth Mindset**
   Building wealth requires a mindset that embraces challenges and views failures as opportunities to learn. A growth mindset keeps you motivated and focused on long-term goals.
8. **Set Clear Goals and Monitor Progress**
   Define your financial goals—whether it's buying a home, starting a business, or retiring early—and track your progress. Regularly review and adjust your strategies as needed.
9. **Leverage Technology**
   Use financial tools and apps to automate savings, track expenses, and gain insights into your spending habits. Technology can simplify and enhance your journey to wealth.
10. **Give Back**
    True wealth includes making a positive impact. Philanthropy not only benefits others but also enriches your life with purpose and satisfaction.

Closing Thoughts

Financial literacy is not a luxury; it is a necessity for navigating life's challenges and achieving your dreams. Whether you're starting from scratch or looking to refine your financial strategies, understanding and applying these principles will set you on a path toward lasting wealth and security. Remember, wealth creation is not a sprint; it's a marathon that rewards patience, perseverance, and informed decision-making. By mastering the fundamentals of financial literacy and embracing the wealth-building process, you can transform your financial future and build a legacy of prosperity.

Chapter 1: Understanding the Basics of Money

Money is an essential component of modern life, shaping our opportunities, decisions, and overall quality of living. Yet, many people operate within the financial system without fully understanding how money works, where it comes from, and how it grows. This chapter delves into the foundational concepts of money, its history, its functions, and how to make it work for you.

What Is Money?

At its core, money is a medium of exchange, a unit of account, and a store of value. It facilitates trade, simplifies transactions, and allows societies to function efficiently. Money has evolved significantly over time, from bartering to coins, paper currency, and now digital forms such as credit, debit, and cryptocurrencies.

- **Medium of Exchange:** Money eliminates the inefficiencies of barter systems, enabling goods and services to be traded easily without requiring a direct exchange of equal value.
- **Unit of Account:** Money provides a standard measure of value, making it easier to compare the worth of different goods and services.
- **Store of Value:** Money retains value over time, allowing individuals to save for future needs or investments.

The History of Money

Understanding money's history provides valuable insights into its role in society:

1. **The Barter System:** The earliest form of trade involved bartering goods and services. While effective in small communities, it posed challenges such as the "double coincidence of wants" (both parties needing what the other offers).
2. **Commodity Money:** Items like salt, shells, or precious metals became widely accepted as currency due to their inherent value.
3. **Metallic Money:** Coins made from gold, silver, and bronze introduced durability and standardization.
4. **Paper Money:** Promissory notes and bank-issued currency represented a shift toward convenience, backed initially by precious metals.
5. **Fiat Money:** Today's money is fiat, meaning it has no intrinsic value but is backed by government authority.
6. **Digital Money:** With technological advances, money now exists in electronic forms, including credit, debit, and cryptocurrencies like Bitcoin.

How Money Works in the Economy

To navigate personal finance effectively, it's essential to understand the broader economic functions of money:

1. **Money Supply:** Central banks control the money supply to influence inflation, employment, and economic growth. Terms like M1, M2, and M3 represent different levels of money in circulation, from cash to deposits.
2. **Inflation and Deflation:** Inflation reduces money's purchasing power, while deflation increases it. Understanding these forces helps you make informed decisions about savings and investments.
3. **Interest Rates:** Interest rates affect borrowing, saving, and investing. Low rates encourage spending and borrowing, while high rates incentivize saving and slow economic growth.
4. **Global Currency Exchange:** In a globalized world, currency values fluctuate based on trade, supply and demand, and geopolitical stability. Knowing exchange rates is crucial for international transactions.

The Psychology of Money

Money is not just a tool; it also represents emotions, values, and beliefs. Your relationship with money—shaped by upbringing, culture, and experiences—impacts how you earn, spend, and save. Common psychological aspects include:

1. **Scarcity Mindset:** A belief in perpetual lack that may hinder financial growth.
2. **Abundance Mindset:** A belief in financial opportunities that encourages proactive wealth-building.
3. **Emotional Spending:** Making purchases based on feelings rather than needs or goals.

The Role of Money in Your Life

To harness money effectively, it's important to clarify its role in your life. Ask yourself:

1. **What Are My Financial Goals?** Whether buying a home, traveling, or retiring early, clear goals give money a purpose.
2. **What Does Money Represent to Me?** Security? Freedom? Power? Understanding this helps you align financial decisions with personal values.
3. **How Do I Feel About Money?** Identifying emotional triggers around money can improve financial habits.

Building a Strong Foundation

Understanding the basics of money begins with mastering these core principles:

1. **Earning Money:**
   - Focus on developing skills and education to increase earning potential.
   - Explore multiple income streams, including side hustles or passive income.
2. **Spending Money Wisely:**
   - Differentiate between needs (essentials) and wants (luxuries).
   - Use budgeting tools to track and control spending.
3. **Saving Money:**
   - Aim to save a portion of every paycheck, even if it's small.
   - Build an emergency fund before focusing on long-term savings.
4. **Investing Money:**
   - Learn about different investment vehicles, such as stocks, bonds, and real estate.
   - Start investing early to take advantage of compound interest.
5. **Managing Debt:**
   - Avoid high-interest debt whenever possible.
   - Pay off existing debts systematically to reduce financial stress.
6. **Protecting Money:**
   - Secure assets with insurance, diversification, and fraud prevention.
   - Plan for the future with retirement accounts and estate planning.

How to Make Money Work for You

Money is a tool to achieve financial independence and security. Here's how to make it work for you:

1. **Leverage Compound Interest:** The earlier you save and invest, the more your money grows exponentially over time.
2. **Create Passive Income:** Focus on generating income that doesn't require constant effort, such as rental properties, dividends, or royalties.
3. **Understand Taxes:** Learn how to minimize tax liabilities through deductions, credits, and strategic planning.
4. **Automate Finances:** Use automation to ensure bills are paid, savings are allocated, and investments grow without requiring daily attention.
5. **Stay Informed:** Regularly update your financial knowledge to adapt to changes in the economy and your personal life.

Closing Thoughts

Understanding the basics of money is not just about learning concepts; it's about cultivating a mindset that views money as a tool for achieving your dreams and securing your future. This chapter lays the groundwork for deeper financial literacy, empowering you to navigate the complexities of personal finance with confidence and clarity. With this foundation, you're ready to move forward on your journey to financial success.

Chapter 2: Developing a Budget That Works

A budget is the blueprint of your financial life. It helps you allocate your resources effectively, track your spending, and achieve your financial goals. Far from being restrictive, a well-designed budget empowers you to take control of your finances, reduce stress, and create opportunities for growth. This chapter guides you through the process of developing a budget that works, tailored to your needs and aspirations.

Why Budgeting Matters

A budget is more than a list of numbers; it's a tool that brings clarity, discipline, and purpose to your financial life. Here's why budgeting matters:

1. **Provides Financial Clarity**
   A budget helps you understand where your money comes from and where it goes, revealing spending patterns and areas for improvement.
2. **Helps Achieve Financial Goals**
   Whether you're saving for a home, paying off debt, or building an emergency fund, a budget ensures your actions align with your goals.
3. **Reduces Financial Stress**
   Knowing you have a plan for your money can alleviate anxiety and uncertainty, especially during financial challenges.
4. **Prevents Overspending**
   A budget sets boundaries, helping you avoid impulsive purchases and stay within your means.
5. **Builds Financial Discipline**
   Regularly tracking and adjusting your budget fosters habits that lead to long-term financial stability.

Steps to Create a Budget That Works

Developing an effective budget involves a clear, step-by-step process tailored to your unique financial situation.

Step 1: Assess Your Current Financial Situation

Before creating a budget, take stock of your financial reality:

1. **Determine Your Income:**
    - Include all sources of income: salary, freelance work, rental income, and side hustles.
    - Use net income (after taxes) for an accurate picture of available funds.
2. **Track Your Expenses:**
    - Categorize expenses into fixed (e.g., rent, utilities) and variable (e.g., dining out, entertainment).
    - Review bank statements, receipts, or use budgeting apps to analyze past spending.
3. **Identify Spending Patterns:**
    - Look for areas where you may be overspending or could cut back.
    - Categorize expenses into needs, wants, and discretionary spending.
4. **Calculate Your Net Cash Flow:**
    - Subtract total expenses from total income.
    - A positive number means you have extra funds; a negative number signals the need for adjustments.

Step 2: Set Clear Financial Goals

A budget is most effective when aligned with your objectives:

1. **Short-Term Goals:**
   - Examples: Building an emergency fund, paying off credit card debt, or saving for a vacation.
2. **Long-Term Goals:**
   - Examples: Buying a home, retiring comfortably, or funding your children's education.
3. **SMART Goals:**
   - Make goals Specific, Measurable, Achievable, Relevant, and Time-bound.

Step 3: Choose a Budgeting Method

There are several budgeting methods to choose from, depending on your preferences and financial needs:

1. **50/30/20 Rule:**
   - Allocate 50% of income to needs, 30% to wants, and 20% to savings or debt repayment.
2. **Zero-Based Budgeting:**
   - Assign every dollar a job, ensuring income minus expenses equals zero.
3. **Envelope System:**
   - Use physical or digital envelopes to allocate funds for specific categories.
4. **Percentage-Based Budgeting:**
   - Set fixed percentages for categories like housing, savings, and leisure.
5. **Pay-Yourself-First Budgeting:**
   - Prioritize saving and investing before allocating funds to other expenses.

Step 4: Build Your Budget

Once you've assessed your finances and chosen a method, it's time to build your budget:

1. **List Income Sources:**
    - Include all monthly income streams.
2. **Categorize Expenses:**
    - Use broad categories such as housing, transportation, groceries, entertainment, and savings.
3. **Set Spending Limits:**
    - Assign realistic amounts to each category based on your past spending and goals.
4. **Account for Irregular Expenses:**
    - Plan for annual expenses like insurance premiums, holiday shopping, or vehicle maintenance.
5. **Include a Miscellaneous Category:**
    - Set aside a small amount for unexpected or unplanned expenses.

Step 5: Track and Adjust

Budgeting is not a one-time task; it requires regular monitoring and adjustments:

1. **Monitor Spending:**
    - Use apps, spreadsheets, or journals to track daily expenses.
2. **Review Monthly Progress:**
    - Compare actual spending to your budget to identify variances.
3. **Adjust as Needed:**
    - Modify spending limits or reallocate funds based on changing circumstances or priorities.
4. **Celebrate Milestones:**
    - Recognize and reward yourself for achieving financial goals, even small ones.

Tips for Sticking to Your Budget

1. **Automate Savings and Payments:**
    - Set up automatic transfers to savings accounts and automatic bill payments to avoid missed deadlines.
2. **Use Cash for Discretionary Spending:**
    - Limit overspending by withdrawing cash for categories like dining out or entertainment.
3. **Limit Impulse Purchases:**
    - Wait 24 hours before making non-essential purchases.
4. **Review Subscriptions:**
    - Cancel unused or unnecessary subscriptions.
5. **Involve the Family:**
    - Share financial goals with family members and work together to stick to the budget.

Common Budgeting Pitfalls and How to Avoid Them

1. **Unrealistic Expectations:**
   - Set achievable limits to avoid frustration and burnout.
2. **Neglecting Irregular Expenses:**
   - Include occasional costs like gifts or medical bills in your budget.
3. **Ignoring Small Expenses:**
   - Track every expense, no matter how minor, as small purchases can add up.
4. **Failing to Revisit the Budget:**
   - Regularly update your budget to reflect changes in income, expenses, or goals.

Budgeting Tools and Resources

1. **Apps:**
   - Tools like Mint, YNAB (You Need A Budget), and EveryDollar simplify budgeting and expense tracking.
2. **Spreadsheets:**
   - Create customized budgets with Excel or Google Sheets templates.
3. **Journals:**
   - For those who prefer analog methods, budgeting journals can be effective.
4. **Financial Coaches or Advisors:**
   - Seek guidance for personalized strategies and accountability.

Closing Thoughts

Developing a budget that works is one of the most empowering steps you can take on your journey to financial freedom. A good budget aligns with your goals, adapts to your circumstances, and provides a clear path toward your aspirations. Remember, budgeting isn't about restriction—it's about intention. By taking control of your finances, you gain the power to shape your future and achieve the life you envision.

Chapter 3: Saving for the Future

Saving for the future is the foundation of financial security and wealth-building. It's not just about setting aside money; it's about creating a system that enables you to achieve both short-term stability and long-term financial independence. In this chapter, we'll explore the importance of saving, strategies to build savings, and how to leverage them to secure your future.

Why Saving for the Future Matters

1. **Financial Security**
   Savings act as a safety net for unexpected expenses, reducing stress and reliance on debt during emergencies like medical bills or job loss.
2. **Achieving Life Goals**
   Whether buying a home, traveling, or funding education, savings help turn dreams into reality.
3. **Building Wealth**
   Consistent saving allows you to invest, taking advantage of compound growth over time.
4. **Preparing for Retirement**
   Saving ensures you have the resources to maintain your lifestyle when you stop working.
5. **Creating Generational Wealth**
   Proper saving and investment strategies can leave a legacy for your family.

Step 1: Understanding the Types of Savings

To save effectively, it's important to understand the different types of savings and their purposes:

1. **Emergency Fund**
    - Covers unexpected expenses like car repairs, medical bills, or temporary unemployment.
    - Goal: 3–6 months' worth of living expenses.
2. **Short-Term Savings**
    - Reserved for expenses within 1–5 years, such as vacations or weddings.
    - Use high-yield savings accounts or certificates of deposit (CDs).
3. **Long-Term Savings**
    - Focused on retirement, homeownership, or children's education.
    - Invested in assets like retirement accounts, stocks, or bonds for growth over time.
4. **Goal-Specific Savings**
    - Allocated for specific purposes like a new car or starting a business.
    - Use separate accounts to track progress.

Step 2: Setting Savings Goals

To save effectively, your goals should be **SMART**: Specific, Measurable, Achievable, Relevant, and Time-bound.

1. **Short-Term Goals:**
    - Example: Save $3,000 in 12 months for a vacation.
    - Plan: Save $250 per month.
2. **Medium-Term Goals:**
    - Example: Save $20,000 in 5 years for a home down payment.
    - Plan: Save $333 per month and invest in low-risk funds.
3. **Long-Term Goals:**
    - Example: Save $1 million for retirement in 30 years.
    - Plan: Contribute consistently to retirement accounts like a 401(k) or IRA.

Step 3: Building the Habit of Saving

Saving doesn't have to be difficult; it requires discipline and the right strategies:

1. **Pay Yourself First**
   - Treat saving as a priority by automating transfers to savings accounts as soon as you receive income.
2. **Start Small, Grow Gradually**
   - Begin with a manageable amount and increase contributions as your income grows.
3. **Automate Savings**
   - Set up automatic transfers to savings or investment accounts to ensure consistency.
4. **Avoid Lifestyle Inflation**
   - As your income increases, maintain or slightly adjust your spending habits to save more.
5. **Track Your Progress**
   - Regularly review savings goals and celebrate milestones to stay motivated.

Step 4: Choosing the Right Savings Tools

Different savings goals require different financial tools. Here's a breakdown:

1. **Savings Accounts**
    - Ideal for short-term savings and emergency funds.
    - Look for high-yield savings accounts for better returns.
2. **Certificates of Deposit (CDs)**
    - Offer higher interest rates than regular savings accounts but require locking in funds for a specific period.
3. **Money Market Accounts**
    - Combine features of savings and checking accounts, often with higher interest rates.
4. **401(k) or 403(b) Plans**
    - Employer-sponsored retirement accounts with tax advantages.
    - Contribute at least enough to get the full employer match if offered.
5. **Individual Retirement Accounts (IRAs)**
    - Tax-advantaged accounts, available in traditional or Roth options.
    - Roth IRA contributions are made post-tax but grow tax-free.
6. **Investment Accounts**
    - Use for long-term savings with potential for higher returns through stocks, bonds, or mutual funds.
7. **Health Savings Accounts (HSAs)**
    - For those with high-deductible health plans, HSAs provide tax-advantaged savings for medical expenses.

Step 5: Overcoming Common Saving Challenges

1. **Living Paycheck to Paycheck**
    - Start small; even saving $5 a week adds up over time.
    - Identify unnecessary expenses to free up cash.
2. **Low Income**
    - Focus on increasing income through side hustles or skill development.
    - Use windfalls like tax refunds for savings.
3. **Lack of Discipline**
    - Automate savings to remove the temptation to spend.
    - Use visual reminders, like progress trackers, to stay motivated.
4. **Unexpected Expenses**
    - Build and maintain an emergency fund to handle unplanned costs.

Step 6: Leveraging the Power of Compound Interest

Compound interest allows your savings to grow exponentially over time. The earlier you start saving, the greater the benefits.

- **Example:**
    - Save $200 monthly at an annual return of 6% starting at age 25: $387,000 by age 65.
    - Starting at age 35 with the same savings: $198,000 by age 65.

Step 7: Protecting Your Savings

1. **Insurance:**
   - Protect assets with health, auto, home, and life insurance to prevent unexpected expenses from depleting savings.
2. **Emergency Fund:**
   - Keep it liquid and easily accessible, but separate from regular spending accounts.
3. **Diversification:**
   - Spread investments across asset types to reduce risk.
4. **Fraud Prevention:**
   - Use secure passwords, monitor accounts regularly, and avoid sharing sensitive information.

Real-Life Saving Strategies

1. **The 24-Hour Rule:**
   - Wait 24 hours before making non-essential purchases to avoid impulsive spending.
2. **Round-Up Savings Apps:**
   - Apps like Acorns round up purchases to the nearest dollar and invest the difference.
3. **Saving Windfalls:**
   - Allocate bonuses, tax refunds, or gifts directly to savings accounts.
4. **Cutting Costs:**
   - Reduce recurring expenses like subscriptions, energy bills, or dining out.

The Emotional Side of Saving

Saving isn't just a financial act; it's an emotional one. Understanding your relationship with money can improve your saving habits:

1. **Recognize Emotional Triggers:**
    - Identify feelings that lead to impulsive spending, such as stress or boredom.
2. **Set Meaningful Goals:**
    - Link savings to goals that resonate emotionally, like family security or dream vacations.
3. **Practice Gratitude:**
    - Focus on what you have rather than what you lack, reducing the urge to overspend.

Closing Thoughts

Saving for the future is a powerful act of self-care and responsibility. By understanding the different types of savings, setting clear goals, and leveraging the right tools, you can build a secure financial future. Remember, saving isn't just about deprivation; it's about empowerment. Every dollar saved is a step closer to financial freedom, peace of mind, and the life you envision. Start small, stay consistent, and watch your efforts compound into a brighter, more secure tomorrow.

Chapter 4: Getting Started with Investments

Investing is a powerful way to grow wealth, achieve financial independence, and secure your future. While saving provides a foundation of security, investing accelerates your financial growth through compounding returns and capital appreciation. This chapter provides an in-depth guide to understanding investments, exploring various types, and building a strategy tailored to your goals and risk tolerance.

Why Investing Matters

1. **Wealth Creation**
   Investments have the potential to grow your money significantly over time, often outpacing inflation and increasing purchasing power.
2. **Achieving Financial Goals**
   Whether planning for retirement, funding education, or building generational wealth, investing provides the means to reach long-term objectives.
3. **Compounding Returns**
   Investments generate returns on both your principal and accumulated earnings, exponentially growing your wealth over time.
4. **Beating Inflation**
   Inflation erodes the value of money. Investing in assets that grow faster than inflation protects your purchasing power.
5. **Passive Income**
   Certain investments, like dividends, rental income, or interest from bonds, can provide additional income streams.

Step 1: Understanding the Basics of Investing

Before diving into investments, it's essential to grasp the fundamental principles:

1. **Risk and Reward**
    - Investments with higher potential returns often carry higher risks. Understanding your risk tolerance is critical to choosing the right assets.
2. **Diversification**
    - Spreading investments across different asset classes (e.g., stocks, bonds, real estate) minimizes risk by reducing reliance on any single investment.
3. **Time Horizon**
    - The amount of time you plan to hold an investment impacts the type of assets you should choose. Longer horizons allow for higher-risk investments with greater growth potential.
4. **Liquidity**
    - Liquidity refers to how quickly an investment can be converted into cash without significant loss of value. Stocks are highly liquid, while real estate is less so.

Step 2: Types of Investments

Understanding the different types of investments is crucial for building a diversified portfolio:

1. **Stocks**
   - Ownership in a company that can grow in value and pay dividends.
   - **Pros:** High growth potential, liquidity, partial ownership.
   - **Cons:** Volatility, potential loss of principal.
2. **Bonds**
   - Loans to governments or corporations that pay fixed interest over time.
   - **Pros:** Stable income, lower risk than stocks.
   - **Cons:** Lower returns, sensitive to interest rates.
3. **Mutual Funds**
   - Pooled funds managed by professionals to invest in diversified assets.
   - **Pros:** Diversification, professional management.
   - **Cons:** Management fees, less control.
4. **Exchange-Traded Funds (ETFs)**
   - Similar to mutual funds but traded on stock exchanges like individual stocks.
   - **Pros:** Low fees, flexibility, diversification.
   - **Cons:** Trading fees, market risk.
5. **Real Estate**
   - Investment in property for rental income or capital appreciation.
   - **Pros:** Tangible asset, passive income, tax benefits.
   - **Cons:** High upfront costs, illiquidity, ongoing management.
6. **Commodities**
   - Physical goods like gold, oil, or agricultural products.
   - **Pros:** Inflation hedge, diversification.

   - **Cons:** Price volatility, no income generation.
7. **Cryptocurrency**
   - Digital assets like Bitcoin and Ethereum.
   - **Pros:** High growth potential, innovation.
   - **Cons:** Extreme volatility, regulatory risks.
8. **Index Funds**
   - Funds that track the performance of a market index (e.g., S&P 500).
   - **Pros:** Low fees, diversification, long-term growth.
   - **Cons:** Limited flexibility, dependent on market performance.
9. **Alternative Investments**
   - Includes private equity, hedge funds, collectibles, and art.
   - **Pros:** High potential returns, diversification.
   - **Cons:** High risk, limited accessibility for beginners.

Step 3: Setting Investment Goals

Investing without a plan can lead to confusion and poor decisions. Define your goals to guide your strategy:

1. **Short-Term Goals:**
   - Example: Saving for a wedding or vacation in 1–3 years.
   - Recommended: Low-risk investments like high-yield savings accounts, CDs, or bonds.
2. **Medium-Term Goals:**
   - Example: Buying a home in 3–10 years.
   - Recommended: Balanced portfolio of stocks and bonds.
3. **Long-Term Goals:**
   - Example: Retirement or wealth building over 10+ years.
   - Recommended: Higher allocation to stocks, index funds, or real estate.

Step 4: Building Your Investment Portfolio

1. **Assess Risk Tolerance:**
    - **High Risk:** Younger investors with long horizons may opt for a stock-heavy portfolio.
    - **Moderate Risk:** A mix of stocks, bonds, and mutual funds balances growth and stability.
    - **Low Risk:** Older investors or those nearing goals may focus on bonds and dividend-paying stocks.
2. **Determine Asset Allocation:**
    - Decide what percentage of your portfolio to allocate to each asset class (e.g., 70% stocks, 20% bonds, 10% cash).
3. **Diversify Across Sectors and Geographies:**
    - Invest in different industries and global markets to minimize risk.
4. **Start Small:**
    - Begin with affordable options like ETFs or fractional shares.

Step 5: Choosing an Investment Platform

The right platform simplifies the investing process. Consider the following:

1. **Brokerage Accounts:**
    - Platforms like Fidelity, Charles Schwab, or Robinhood offer a wide range of investment options.
2. **Retirement Accounts:**
    - 401(k), IRA, or Roth IRA accounts offer tax advantages for long-term savings.
3. **Robo-Advisors:**
    - Automated platforms like Betterment or Wealthfront manage investments based on your goals and risk tolerance.
4. **Apps:**
    - Beginner-friendly apps like Acorns or Stash allow small, incremental investments.

Step 6: Strategies for Successful Investing

1. **Start Early:**
   - Time is your most valuable asset. Begin investing as soon as possible to maximize compounding.
2. **Invest Regularly:**
   - Use dollar-cost averaging to invest a fixed amount at regular intervals, reducing the impact of market volatility.
3. **Reinvest Earnings:**
   - Reinvest dividends and interest to accelerate growth.
4. **Monitor and Adjust:**
   - Review your portfolio regularly to ensure it aligns with your goals and market conditions.
5. **Avoid Emotional Decisions:**
   - Base investment choices on data and strategy, not fear or greed.
6. **Focus on Long-Term Growth:**
   - Avoid frequent trading, which can incur fees and reduce returns.

Step 7: Avoiding Common Investment Pitfalls

1. **Chasing Trends:**
   - Avoid investing in "hot" stocks or assets without proper research.
2. **Neglecting Diversification:**
   - Concentrating investments in one sector or stock increases risk.
3. **Timing the Market:**
   - Predicting market movements is risky and often leads to losses.
4. **Overlooking Fees:**
   - Pay attention to management and transaction fees, which can erode returns.
5. **Ignoring Inflation:**
   - Ensure your investments outpace inflation to maintain purchasing power.

Step 8: The Role of Professional Guidance

For beginners or complex financial situations, consider professional advice:

1. **Financial Advisors:**
   - Provide personalized guidance based on your goals and circumstances.
2. **Certified Financial Planners (CFPs):**
   - Offer comprehensive planning, including tax strategies and estate planning.
3. **Investment Managers:**
   - Handle large portfolios for those who prefer a hands-off approach.

Closing Thoughts

Getting started with investments can seem intimidating, but with knowledge and a clear plan, you can navigate the financial markets with confidence. Remember, investing is not about quick wins but building long-term wealth. Start small, stay consistent, and let time and discipline work in your favor. With a diversified portfolio and a commitment to learning, you'll be well on your way to achieving financial independence.

Chapter 5: Building Financial Confidence

Financial confidence is the ability to navigate your financial life with clarity, competence, and resilience. It's about more than just knowing the numbers—it's about trusting yourself to make sound decisions, adapt to changes, and take control of your financial future. In this chapter, we'll explore strategies to build financial confidence, address common fears, and empower you to approach money with a growth mindset.

Why Financial Confidence Matters

1. **Empowers Decision-Making**
   Financial confidence gives you the ability to make informed choices about spending, saving, investing, and debt management without second-guessing yourself.
2. **Reduces Stress**
   When you feel in control of your finances, you're less likely to experience anxiety about money or the future.
3. **Improves Financial Health**
   Confident individuals are more likely to stick to budgets, save regularly, and pursue wealth-building opportunities.
4. **Encourages Risk-Taking**
   Financial confidence allows you to explore new opportunities, such as investing or starting a business, with calculated risks.
5. **Strengthens Resilience**
   Confident individuals bounce back more easily from financial setbacks, adapting and learning from challenges.

Step 1: Understand Your Financial Starting Point

Confidence begins with clarity. To build financial confidence, you must first understand where you stand financially:

1. **Calculate Net Worth**
   - Add up all your assets (e.g., savings, investments, property) and subtract liabilities (e.g., loans, credit card debt).
2. **Evaluate Cash Flow**
   - Assess your monthly income and expenses to identify areas of surplus or shortfall.
3. **Analyze Spending Habits**
   - Review past transactions to uncover patterns and opportunities for improvement.
4. **Identify Financial Strengths and Weaknesses**
   - Acknowledge what you're doing well and where you need to grow.

Step 2: Overcome Common Financial Fears

Fear and doubt are major barriers to financial confidence. Confronting these fears head-on is essential:

1. **Fear of Failure**
    - **Solution:** Treat financial mistakes as learning opportunities. Every successful investor, saver, or entrepreneur has faced setbacks.
2. **Fear of Complexity**
    - **Solution:** Break financial concepts into manageable parts. Focus on mastering one topic (e.g., budgeting) before moving to the next.
3. **Fear of Risk**
    - **Solution:** Educate yourself about risk management and start small with lower-risk financial decisions.
4. **Fear of Scarcity**
    - **Solution:** Cultivate an abundance mindset by focusing on opportunities to grow your income and assets.

Step 3: Develop a Growth Mindset

A growth mindset is essential for building financial confidence. It helps you view challenges as opportunities to learn rather than insurmountable obstacles.

1. **Embrace Lifelong Learning**
    - Continuously educate yourself about personal finance through books, podcasts, courses, and workshops.
2. **Set Realistic Expectations**
    - Understand that building wealth and confidence is a gradual process, not an overnight success.
3. **Focus on Progress, Not Perfection**
    - Celebrate small wins, such as sticking to your budget for a month or increasing your savings rate.
4. **Practice Gratitude**
    - Reflect on what you've achieved and the resources you already have, fostering a sense of empowerment.

Step 4: Build Financial Knowledge

Knowledge is a key driver of confidence. The more you understand about personal finance, the more empowered you'll feel:

1. **Master the Basics**
    - Learn about budgeting, saving, investing, and debt management.
2. **Understand Your Financial Tools**
    - Familiarize yourself with the accounts, credit cards, and investment platforms you use.
3. **Stay Informed**
    - Keep up with financial news and trends to understand how economic changes might affect you.
4. **Ask Questions**
    - Don't hesitate to seek clarification from professionals or trusted resources when something is unclear.

Step 5: Take Small, Consistent Actions

Confidence grows through action. Small, consistent steps build momentum and reinforce positive habits:

1. **Automate Savings**
   - Set up automatic transfers to savings or investment accounts to ensure consistent progress.
2. **Track Your Progress**
   - Use apps, spreadsheets, or journals to monitor your financial journey.
3. **Address One Issue at a Time**
   - Focus on tackling one financial challenge (e.g., reducing debt) before moving to the next.
4. **Revisit and Adjust Goals**
   - Regularly review your financial goals and make adjustments as needed.

Step 6: Surround Yourself with Support

The people around you can significantly impact your financial confidence. Build a supportive network:

1. **Seek Mentors**
    - Connect with financially savvy individuals who can share insights and guidance.
2. **Join Financial Communities**
    - Participate in online forums, social media groups, or local meetups focused on personal finance.
3. **Engage Family and Friends**
    - Share your financial goals with trusted individuals for accountability and encouragement.
4. **Work with Professionals**
    - Consider hiring a financial advisor or coach to help you develop and execute a plan.

Step 7: Cultivate Healthy Financial Habits

Habits shape your financial life. Building healthy financial routines fosters long-term confidence:

1. **Budget Regularly**
    - Review and adjust your budget monthly to reflect changes in income or expenses.
2. **Save Consistently**
    - Commit to saving a percentage of every paycheck, no matter how small.
3. **Review Credit Reports**
    - Check your credit report regularly to ensure accuracy and address issues promptly.
4. **Invest Gradually**
    - Start with small investments and increase contributions as you become more confident.
5. **Limit Impulse Spending**
    - Pause before making non-essential purchases to ensure they align with your priorities.

Step 8: Measure and Celebrate Progress

Recognizing achievements reinforces confidence and motivation:

1. **Set Milestones:**
    - Break goals into smaller, measurable steps (e.g., saving $1,000, then $5,000).
2. **Track Results:**
    - Use tools like net worth trackers or savings calculators to visualize progress.
3. **Reward Yourself:**
    - Celebrate milestones with affordable rewards, like a favorite treat or activity.
4. **Reflect on Growth:**
    - Compare where you started with where you are now to appreciate how far you've come.

Common Challenges in Building Financial Confidence

1. **Imposter Syndrome**
    - **Solution:** Remind yourself that financial growth is a journey, and everyone starts somewhere.
2. **Setbacks**
    - **Solution:** Treat setbacks as temporary and focus on actionable steps to recover.
3. **Information Overload**
    - **Solution:** Stick to reputable sources and focus on one topic at a time.
4. **Peer Pressure**
    - **Solution:** Stay focused on your goals and avoid comparing yourself to others.

Closing Thoughts

Building financial confidence is a transformative process that empowers you to take charge of your financial future. By understanding your current situation, overcoming fears, developing a growth mindset, and taking consistent action, you'll cultivate the skills and resilience needed to navigate any financial challenge. Confidence is not built overnight, but with patience, education, and persistence, you can achieve a sense of financial security and freedom that will positively impact every aspect of your life.

Appendix A: Budget Templates and Financial Calculators

This appendix provides practical tools and resources to help you apply the financial principles discussed in this book. Budget templates and financial calculators are invaluable aids for tracking expenses, setting financial goals, and making informed decisions. Use the templates and calculators outlined here to simplify your financial planning and build confidence in managing your money.

Budget Templates

A well-designed budget template helps you allocate your income effectively, monitor expenses, and achieve your financial goals. Below are several templates tailored to different needs:

1. Monthly Budget Template

Purpose: Track monthly income and expenses.

Category	Planned Amount	Actual Amount	Difference
Income			
Salary/Wages			
Freelance/ Side Hustle			
Investments			
Total Income			
Expenses			

Category	Planned Amount	Actual Amount	Difference
Housing (Rent/Mortgage)			
Utilities			
Groceries			
Transportation			
Entertainment			
Insurance			
Savings			
Debt Payments			
Miscellaneous			
Total Expenses			
Net Savings			

2. 50/30/20 Budget Template

Purpose: Allocate income according to the 50% needs, 30% wants, and 20% savings rule.

Category	Planned Amount	Actual Amount	Percentage of Income
Needs (50%)			
Rent/Mortgage			
Utilities			
Groceries			
Transportation			
Insurance			
Wants (30%)			
Dining Out			
Entertainment			
Subscriptions			
Travel			
Savings (20%)			
Emergency Fund			
Investments			

Category	Planned Amount	Actual Amount	Percentage of Income
Retirement Savings			

3. Debt Repayment Plan Template

Purpose: Organize and track progress on paying off debts.

Debt Name	Balance	Interest Rate	Minimum Payment	Extra Payment	New Balance
Credit Card 1					
Credit Card 2					
Student Loan					
Auto Loan					
Personal Loan					
Total					

4. Savings Goal Tracker

Purpose: Monitor progress toward specific financial goals.

Goal	Target Amount	Deadline	Current Amount Saved	Monthly Contribution	Progress (%)
Emergency Fund					
Down Payment					
Vacation Fund					
Retirement Savings					

5. Annual Expense Overview

Purpose: Review yearly expenses and identify trends.

Category	Planned Annual Expense	Actual Annual Expense	Difference
Housing (Rent/Mortgage)			
Utilities			
Transportation			
Insurance			
Groceries			
Debt Payments			
Entertainment			
Travel			
Savings			
Miscellaneous			

Financial Calculators

Financial calculators simplify complex calculations, enabling you to plan effectively and make informed decisions. Below are some key calculators and how to use them.

1. Compound Interest Calculator

Purpose: Estimate the growth of savings or investments over time.

Formula:

A=P×(1+r/n)n×tA = P \times (1 + r/n)^{n \times t}A=P×(1+r/n)n×t
Where:

- AAA: Future value of investment
- PPP: Initial principal
- rrr: Annual interest rate (decimal)
- nnn: Number of times interest is compounded per year
- ttt: Time in years

Example:

- Initial savings: $10,000
- Annual interest rate: 5% (0.05)
- Compounded annually: 1 time/year
- Time: 10 years

A=10,000×(1+0.05/1)1×10=$16,288.95A = 10,000 \times (1 + 0.05/1)^{1 \times 10} = \$16,288.95A=10,000×(1+0.05/1)1×10=$16,288.95

2. Retirement Savings Calculator

Purpose: Determine how much you need to save to meet retirement goals.

Inputs:

- Current age
- Retirement age
- Current savings
- Monthly savings contribution
- Expected annual return rate

Output:

- Total savings at retirement
- Monthly income during retirement

3. Debt Payoff Calculator

Purpose: Calculate the time and interest needed to pay off debts.

Inputs:

- Loan balance
- Interest rate
- Monthly payment amount

Output:

- Total interest paid
- Time to payoff

4. Budget Percentage Calculator

Purpose: Allocate income according to budget categories (e.g., 50/30/20 rule).

Inputs:

- Monthly income
- Percentages for needs, wants, and savings

Output:

- Dollar amounts for each category

5. Savings Goal Calculator

Purpose: Determine how long it will take to reach a savings goal.

Inputs:

- Goal amount
- Current savings
- Monthly contribution
- Annual interest rate

Output:

- Time to achieve goal

How to Access and Use These Tools

1. **Spreadsheet Software:**
   - Use platforms like Microsoft Excel or Google Sheets to customize templates and perform calculations.
2. **Online Calculators:**
   - Websites like Investor.gov and Bankrate offer free financial calculators.
3. **Mobile Apps:**
   - Apps like Mint, YNAB (You Need a Budget), and Personal Capital include built-in calculators and budget tracking features.
4. **Financial Software:**
   - Consider tools like Quicken or QuickBooks for advanced budgeting and financial planning.

Closing Thoughts

Budget templates and financial calculators are essential tools for managing your finances effectively. They provide clarity, streamline decision-making, and help you stay accountable to your financial goals. Use these resources regularly to monitor your progress, adjust your plans, and build lasting financial confidence.

Message from the Author:

I hope you enjoyed this book, I love astrology and knew there was not a book such as this out on the shelf. I love metaphysical items as well. Please check out my other books:

-Life of Government Benefits

-My life of Hell

-My life with Hydrocephalus

-Red Sky

-World Domination:Woman's rule

-World Domination:Woman's Rule 2: The War

-Life and Banishment of Apophis: book 1

-The Kidney Friendly Diet

-The Ultimate Hemp Cookbook

-Creating a Dispensary(legally)

-Cleanliness throughout life: the importance of showering from childhood to adulthood.

-Strong Roots: The Risks of Overcoddling children

-Hemp Horoscopes: Cosmic Insights and Earthly Healing

- Celestial Hemp Navigating the Zodiac: Through the Green Cosmos

-Astrological Hemp: Aligning The Stars with Earth's Ancient Herb

-The Astrological Guide to Hemp: Stars, Signs, and Sacred Leaves

-Green Growth: Innovative Marketing Strategies for your Hemp Products and Dispensary

-Cosmic Cannabis

-Astrological Munchies

-Henry The Hemp

-Zodiacal Roots: The Astrological Soul Of Hemp

- **Green Constellations: Intersection of Hemp and Zodiac**

-Hemp in The Houses: An astrological Adventure Through The Cannabis Galaxy

-Galactic Ganja Guide

Heavenly Hemp

Zodiac Leaves

Doctor Who Astrology

Cannastrology

Stellar Satvias and Cosmic Indicas

Celestial Cannabis: A Zodiac Journey

AstroHerbology: The Sky and The Soil: Volume 1

AstroHerbology:Celestial Cannabis:Volume 2

Cosmic Cannabis Cultivation

The Starry Guide to Herbal Harmony: Volume 1

The Starry Guide to Herbal Harmony: Cannabis Universe: Volume 2

Yugioh Astrology: Astrological Guide to Deck, Duels and more

Nightmare Mansion: Echoes of The Abyss

Nightmare Mansion 2: Legacy of Shadows

Nightmare Mansion 3: Shadows of the Forgotten

Nightmare Mansion 4: Echoes of the Damned

The Life and Banishment of Apophis: Book 2

Nightmare Mansion: Halls of Despair

Healing with Herb: Cannabis and Hydrocephalus

Planetary Pot: Aligning with Astrological Herbs: Volume 1

Fast Track to Freedom: 30 Days to Financial Independence Using AI, Assets, and Agile Hustles

Cosmic Hemp Pathways

How to Become Financially Free in 30 Days: 10,000 Paths to Prosperity

Zodiacal Herbage: Astrological Insights: Volume 1

Nightmare Mansion: Whispers in the Walls

The Daleks Invade Atlantis

Henry the hemp and Hydrocephalus

10X The Kidney Friendly Diet

Cannabis Universe: Adult coloring book

Hemp Astrology: The Healing Power of the Stars

Zodiacal Herbage: Astrological Insights: Cannabis Universe: Volume 2

Planetary Pot: Aligning with Astrological Herbs: Cannabis Universes: Volume 2

Doctor Who Meets the Replicators and SG-1: The Ultimate Battle for Survival

Nightmare Mansion: Curse of the Blood Moon

The Celestial Stoner: A Guide to the Zodiac

Cosmic Pleasures: Sex Toy Astrology for Every Sign

Hydrocephalus Astrology: Navigating the Stars and Healing Waters

Lapis and the Mischievous Chocolate Bar

Celestial Positions: Sexual Astrology for Every Sign

Apophis's Shadow Work Journal: **:** A Journey of Self-Discovery and Healing

Kinky Cosmos: Sexual Kink Astrology for Every Sign

Digital Cosmos: The Astrological Digimon Compendium

Stellar Seeds: The Cosmic Guide to Growing with Astrology

Apophis's Daily Gratitude Journal

Cat Astrology: Feline Mysteries of the Cosmos

The Cosmic Kama Sutra: An Astrological Guide to Sexual Positions

Unleash Your Potential: A Guided Journal Powered by AI Insights

Whispers of the Enchanted Grove

Cosmic Pleasures: An Astrological Guide to Sexual Kinks

369, 12 Manifestation Journal

Whisper of the nocturne journal(blank journal for writing or drawing)

The Boogey Book

Locked In Reflection: A Chastity Journey Through Locktober

Generating Wealth Quickly:

How to Generate $100,000 in 24 Hours

Star Magic: Harness the Power of the Universe

The Flatulence Chronicles: A Fart Journal for Self-Discovery

The Doctor and The Death Moth

Seize the Day: A Personal Seizure Tracking Journal

The Ultimate Boogeyman Safari: A Journey into the Boogie World and Beyond

Whispers of Samhain: 1,000 Spells of Love, Luck, and Lunar Magic: Samhain Spell Book

Apophis's guides:

Witch's Spellbook Crafting Guide for Halloween

Frost & Flame: The Enchanted Yule Grimoire of 1000 Winter Spells

The Ultimate Boogey Goo Guide & Spooky Activities for Halloween Fun

Harmony of the Scales: A Libra's Spellcraft for Balance and Beauty

The Enchanted Advent: 36 Days of Christmas Wonders

Nightmare Mansion: The Labyrinth of Screams

Harvest of Enchantment: 1,000 Spells of Gratitude, Love, and Fortune for Thanksgiving

The Boogey Chronicles: A Journal of Nightly Encounters and Shadowy Secrets

The 12 Days of Financial Freedom: A Step-by-Step Christmas Countdown to Transform Your Finances

Sigil of the Eternal Spiral Blank Journal

A Christmas Feast: Timeless Recipes for Every Meal

Holiday Stress-Free Solutions: A Survival Guide to Thriving During the Festive Season

Yu-Gi-Oh! Holiday Gifting Mastery: The Ultimate Guide for Fans and Newcomers Alike

Holiday Harmony: A Hydrocephalus Survival Guide for the Festive Season

Celestial Craft: The Witch's Almanac for 2025 – A Cosmic Guide to Manifestations, Moons, and Mystical Events

Doctor Who: The Toymaker's Winter Wonderland

Tulsa King Unveiled: A Thrilling Guide to Stallone's Mafia Masterpiece

Pendulum Craft: A Complete Guide to Crafting and Using Personalized Divination Tools

Nightmare Mansion: Santa's Eternal Eve

Starlight Noel: A Cosmic Journey through Christmas Mysteries

The Dark Architect: Unlocking the Blueprint of Existence

Surviving the Embrace: The Ultimate Guide to Encounters with The Hugging Molly

The Enchanted Codex: Secrets of the Craft for Witches, Wiccans, and Pagans

Harvest of Gratitude: A Complete Thanksgiving Guide

Yuletide Essentials: A Complete Guide to an Authentic and Magical Christmas

Celestial Smokes: A Cosmic Guide to Cigars and Astrology

Living in Balance: A Comprehensive Survival Guide to Thriving with Diabetes Insipidus

Cosmic Symbiosis: The Venom Zodiac Chronicles

The Cursed Paw of Ambition

Cosmic Symbiosis: The Astrological Venom Journal

Celestial Wonders Unfold: A Stargazer's Guide to the Cosmos (2024-2029)

The Ultimate Black Friday Prepper's Guide: Mastering Shopping Strategies and Savings

Cosmic Sales: The Astrological Guide to Black Friday Shopping
Legends of the Corn Mother and Other Harvest Myths
Whispers of the Harvest: The Corn Mother's Journal
The Evergreen Spellbook
The Doctor Meets the Boogeyman
The White Witch of Rose Hall's SpellBook
The Gingerbread Golem's Shadow: A Study in Sweet Darkness
The Gingerbread Golem Codex: An Academic Exploration of Sweet Myths
The Gingerbread Golem Grimoire: Sweet Magicks and Spells for the Festive Witch
The Curse of the Gingerbread Golem
10-minute Christmas Crafts for kids
Christmas Crisis Solutions: The Ultimate Last-Minute Survival Guide
Gingerbread Golem Recipes: Holiday Treats with a Magical Twist
The Infinite Key: Unlocking Mystical Secrets of the Ages
Enchanted Yule: A Wiccan and Pagan Guide to a Magical and Memorable Season
Dinosaurs of Power: Unlocking Ancient Magick
Astro-Dinos: The Cosmic Guide to Prehistoric Wisdom
Gallifrey's Yule Logs: A Festive Doctor Who Cookbook
The Dino Grimoire: Secrets of Prehistoric Magick
The Gift They Never Knew They Needed
The Gingerbread Golem's Culinary Alchemy: Enchanting Recipes for a Sweetly Dark Feast
A Time Lord Christmas: Holiday Adventures with the Doctor
Krampusproofing Your Home: Defensive Strategies for Yule
Silent Frights: A Collection of Christmas Creepypastas to Chill Your Bones
Santa Raptor's Jolly Carnage: A Dino-Claus Christmas Tale
Prehistoric Palettes: A Dino Wicca Coloring Journey
The Christmas Wishkeeper Chronicles

The Starlight Sleigh: A Holiday Journey
Elf Secrets: The True Magic of the North Pole
Candy Cane Conjurations
Cooking with Kids: Recipes Under 20 Minutes
Doctor Who: The TARDIS Confiscation
The Anxiety First Aid Kit: Quick Tools to Calm Your Mind
Frosty Whispers: A Winter's Tale
The Infinite Key: Unlocking the Secrets to Prosperity, Resilience, and Purpose
The Grasping Void: Why You'll Regret This Purchase
Astrology for Busy Bees: Star Signs Simplified
The Instant Focus Formula: Cut Through the Noise
The Secret Language of Colors: Unlocking the Emotional Codes
Sacred Fossil Chronicles: Blank Journal
The Christmas Cottage Miracle
Feeding Frenzy: Graboid-Inspired Recipes
Manifest in Minutes: The Quick Law of Attraction Guide
The Symbiote Chronicles: Doctor Who's Venomous Journey
Think Tiny, Grow Big: The Minimalist Mindset
The Energy Key: Unlocking Limitless Motivation
New Year, New Magic: Manifesting Your Best Year Yet
Unstoppable You: Mastering Confidence in Minutes
Infinite Energy: The Secret to Never Feeling Drained
Lightning Focus: Mastering the Art of Productivity in a Distracted World
Saturnalia Manifestation Magick: A Guide to Unlocking Abundance During the Solstice
Graboids and Garland: The Ultimate Tremors-Themed Christmas Guide
12 Nights of Holiday Magic
The Power of Pause: 60-Second Mindfulness Practices
The Quick Reset: How to Reclaim Your Life After Burnout
The Shadow Eater: A Tale of Despair and Survival

The Micro-Mastery Method: Transform Your Skills in Just Minutes a Day

Reclaiming Time: How to Live More by Doing Less

Chronovore: The Eternal Nexus

The Mind Reset: Unlocking Your Inner Peace in a Chaotic World

Confidence Code: Building Unshakable Self-Belief

Baby the Vampire Terrier

Baby the Vampire Terrier's Christmas Adventure

Celestial Streams: The Content Creator's Astrology Manual

The Wealth Whisperer: Unlocking Abundance with Everyday Actions

The Energy Equation: Maximize Your Output Without Burning Out

The Happiness Algorithm: Science-Backed Steps to Joyful Living

Stress-Free Success: Achieving Goals Without Anxiety

Mindful Wealth: The New Blueprint for Financial Freedom

The Festive Flavors of New Year: A Culinary Celebration

The Master's Gambit: Keys of Eternal Power

Shadowed Secrets: Groundhog Day Mysteries

Beneath the Burrow: Lessons from the Groundhog

Spring's Whispers: The Groundhog's Prediction

The Limitless Mindset: Unlock Your Untapped Potential

The Focus Funnel: How to Cut Through Chaos and Get Results

Bold Moves: Building Courage to Live on Your Terms

The Daily Shift: Simple Practices for Lasting Transformation

The Quarter-Life Reset: Thriving in Your 20s and 30s

The Art of Shadowplay: Building Your Own Personal Myth

The Eternal Loop: Finding Purpose in Repetition

Burrowing Wisdom: Life Lessons from the Groundhog

Shadow Work: A Groundhog Day Perspective

Love in Bloom: 5-Minute Romantic Gestures

The Shadowspell Codex: Secrets of Forbidden Magick

The Burnout Cure: Finding Balance in a Busy World

The Groundhog Prophecy: Unlocking Seasonal Secrets
Nog Tales: The Spirited History of Eggnog
Six More Weeks: Embracing Seasonal Transitions
The Lumivian Chronicles: Fragments of the Fifth Dimension

Get Some Tarot cards: https://www.makeplayingcards.com/sell/apophis-occult-shop

Get some shirts: https://www.bonfire.com/store/apophis-shirt-emporium/

Instagrams:
@apophis_enterprises,
@apophisbookemporium,
@apophisscardshop
Twitter: @apophisenterpr1
Tiktok:@apophisenterprise
Youtube: @sg1fan23477, @FiresideRetreatKingdom
Hive: @sg1fan23477
CheeLee: @SG1fan23477

Podcast: Apophis Chat Zone: https://open.spotify.com/show/5zXbrCLEV2xzCp8ybrfHsk?si=fb4d4fdbdce44dec

Newsletter: https://apophiss-newsletter-27c897.beehiiv.com/

If you want to support me or see posts of other projects that I have come over to: **buymeacoffee.com/mpetchinskg**

I post there daily several times a day

Get your Dinowicca or Christmas themed digital products, especially Santa Raptor songs and other musics. Here: **https://sg1fan23477.gumroad.com**

Apophis Yuletide Digital has not only digital Christmas items, but it will have all things with Dinowicca as well as other Digital products.

www.ingramcontent.com/pod-product-compliance
Lightning Source LLC
LaVergne TN
LVHW022025200926
848481LV00007B/2549